THE RAZ/SHUMAKER PRAIRIE SCHOONER BOOK PRIZE IN POETRY

Editor: Kwame Dawes

DEAR

DIASPORA

SUSAN NGUYEN

UNIVERSITY OF NEBRASKA PRESS   LINCOLN

Acknowledgments for the use of previously
published material appear on page 61, which
constitutes an extension of the copyright page.

Library of Congress Cataloging-in-Publication Data
Names: Nguyen, Susan, 1992– author.
Title: Dear diaspora / Susan Nguyen.
Description: Lincoln: University of Nebraska
Press, [2021] | Series: The Raz/Shumaker
Prairie Schooner Book Prize in poetry
Identifiers: LCCN 2021010561
ISBN 9781496227904 (paperback)
ISBN 9781496229267 (epub)
ISBN 9781496229274 (pdf)
Subjects: LCGFT: Poetry.
Classification: LCC PS3614.G958 D43
2021 | DDC 811/.6—dc23
LC record available at https://lccn.loc.gov/2021010561

Designed and set in Garamond Premier Pro by L. Auten.

for my mother, for my father

Why resurrect it all now. From the Past. History, the old wound. The past emotions all over again. To confess to relive the same folly. To name it now so as not to repeat history in oblivion. To extract each fragment by each fragment from the word from the image another word another image the reply that will not repeat history in oblivion.

Theresa Hak Kyung Cha, *Dictee*

CONTENTS

DEAR DIASPORA

The Body as a Series of Questions:

What did you leave when crossing the bridge? From what materials was the
   bridge constructed?

   When did you first recoil

          from your mouth?   Do you feel safe wrecking language?

What movie theatre did you travel through? What apple?

   Face?
      Rubber band?
          Onion?   Pocket?

          Can you list the responsibilities of a needle?

When did you lose the color green? The small fire of pennies?

   How did you get it back?

                   Why did you bury the puddle?

   At the center of your calamity, what grows?

No

The tongue diving into dark: fish, sinking stone

   vibrating against your torso   smoothing away the ground

          where the body washes away

I was running fast because of what was behind me   the bridge existed a few steps
before me then disappeared   through wooden slats rose the sound of rainwater
   I absorbed the sound until there was nothing else

because it licked at my face

because it peeled back the sidewalk and showed me rivers of light

because I sustained injuries

because my tongue leapt at sound

A sharp eye that pierces

By the subway station, fourteen red doors, in the neighbor's backyard, pale and still, fro
a jar, in the vegetable drawer, lined or unlined, embroidered and blue

that summer I was always looking up   looking through trees, their blemished arm
    the green was something inside me   it existed at certain hours when I
opened myself   when everything that landed on me weighed nothing   a sma
leaf, green and fleshy   something to put in my mouth

No

It took a mallet   It took a hammer   pummel strike   nail

It took pine spruce   birch elm cherry oak ash   soil toil   It took

My tongue, glowing pink. Shivering like a lure.

???

The First Language

i.

Behind the church we ran through labyrinths of poplar and hickory, dirt paths cutting through ravines and the backs of suburban homes, their brick patios and striped furniture.

In the green light of summer, we loved getting lost, how we could step into woods and exit in a cul-de-sac eight blocks away, loved it best when tadpoles formed a halo around our toes.

ii.

Before he disappeared, my father taught me how to catch tadpoles in my hand. The trick wasn't just to stay still but to stop breathing. He caught dozens like this, knees bent and pant legs folded, his face inches above the creek.

He taught me that our first language was named after tadpoles, the way they moved through water: a knife dissecting the stratosphere, a voice cutting quiet.

iii.

My third-favorite memory of him is walking hand in hand on two-lane roads, identifying Virginia trees.

In one pocket a zodiac-sign lighter, a button from Mother's favorite blouse. In the other: acorns for burying.

I can still identify the red oaks.

iv.

Today the tadpoles flow through my fingers like an egg yolk, and my impulse is to cradle one in my mouth: the tadpole swims circles and my tongue follows, mapping its movement before spitting.

Suzi with an *i*

is not afraid of the dark or the things that move in its current. She approaches school like she approaches most things: eyes narrowed scanning the edges of sight. When she scribbles her name, she dots the *i*, rubs the sharp graphite onto her finger. Before bed she says *OurFatherOurFatherOurFatherOurFather* as fast as she can. The fastest was in Sunday School. Highlighting the Virgin Mary pink, she drowned out the counselor's drone with prayer. Tonight she turns her blinds inward. Through a tiny sliver, the moon spoils the dark.

Suzi's Mother Does Nails

and comes home smelling like acrylic, hair limp, deflated like a paper bag. For her birthday, Suzi's mother and her nail lady friends sit on the front steps, give out French manicures in between Lucky Strike puffs. *In France they call this la French.* Suzi's mother doesn't allow sleepovers. *What if something happens to these white girls? How would that look? The neighbors won't mow our lawn.* The mothers come at 8 sharp and skim their daughters' nails, their tongue inside their cheeks like a hard gumball. *We've never been to this part of town before.*

Letter to the Diaspora

Dear Diaspora,

~~I believe in the american dream~~

last night I had the american dream

in the dream I had an indoor pool

in the dream I walked my dead dog with a diamond leash

        I ate a greasy burger with my perfect hands

        I had the most beautiful sex

        my skin was smooth   alabaster as the moon

in the morning everything had changed

there was no pool   only twine for drying clothes

the dead remained dead

my perfect hands held nothing

nothing was better

The Last Time She Saw Him

was after dinner washing the dishes. Her mother had brought home rice vermicelli soup and paddy crabs. This wasn't her father's first disappearance. Sometimes Suzi couldn't tell when he disappeared from when he left for fishing trips on the coast, when he stayed out all night and went to work after sleeping in the car or no sleep at all. But always he materialized in a few days or a week. From the broken-down cardboard boxes and crushed pistachios in his car, $1 scratch-offs and green, green grass emerged her father: dark and sinewy, mouth full of resin.

Cicada Summer

The cicadas come from the ground and enter
the world in currents, streaming down tree trunks,
over branches, across sidewalks and roads, the males
pulsing their abdomens, singing for sex. In the field
behind the school, Suzi and her classmates stand
still as dozens climb over their bodies, careful not to crush
the winged insects beneath their feet, fearful of littering
the ground with broken glass. Suzi collects every wing
she can find: each one becomes a small body
of water she carries in her pocket, a broken window
pane she holds to each eye. She counts dozens more
on her way home and imagines how they would taste.
Hands in her pockets, touching the wings to each fingertip,
she wonders: would they still sing on the way to death,
and would it sound any different? Today she walks
through uneven fields of green and spits into tall grass,
the roots of trees—listens as the clicking of cicadas
fills her body with song. The green lacerates her ankles,
and she imagines her blood mixed with dirt will nourish,
will add to the muscle tremor of the earth.

Beast Angel

after Eduardo C. Corral

In sleep you come to me with a ball of yarn,
      bind my palms into prayer. From your arm

emerges a swarm of bees. You are carried
      by their sound. Your body shivers

with buzzing. I pray for silence, for ecstasy,
      not knowing its name. You float over fields of needle grass,

each toe a quivering arrow through the green
      of morning. In this light, I open the garden of my body.

Let loose hunger. Let loose the nest of field mice
      and the coiled snake. In this light, I pray

to hold stillness like a gun.

If I Say My Body Is Grieving

after Athena Farrokhzad

Is it American or Vietnamese?

My mother said: Our country no longer exists
My father said: In our language, the same word means green and blue: *xanh*

My father said: To distinguish between the two,
you say *xanh lá*: green leaf, and *xanh da trời*: blue sky

My mother's miscarriage-after-me said: What color was I?

My mother said: In our language, the same word means land and water: *nước*
My grandmother said: All of language is a metaphor   Say what you mean

My father said: If I say I cannot live without *nước*, do I mean country?

My mother said: Vietnam's body curves like the letter *S*: serpentine, fragile

My father said: The Mekong Delta translates to River of Nine Dragons because nine
tributaries sprawl toward the sea

My mother's miscarriage-after-me said: Was my salted mouth American or Vietnamese?

My mother said: Don't translate me

My grandmother said: Don't speak lest your tongue rush like a river

In the night, history absconds with us
We learn to open in darkness

My mother said: When you tell it, do I float on land and water?
My father said: Am I the green leaf   the blue sky?

My American mouth cannot separate itself from my body

Wish List

Suzi plucks the occasional white hair from her mother's head and all the stiff hairs from her powdered armpit. Each dozen is worth a dime. This is her only allowance. She used to pluck her father's white hairs too, but when they spread to his sideburns and eyebrows, her mother bought black hair dye from cvs.

When Suzi first asks for an allowance, her mother doesn't know the meaning of the word. *Who pays for your food? Gives you a roof to sleep under?* The next day she tells all her nail lady friends, who whoop for days. *And who raised her like that?*

Suzi adds *allowance* to her Wish List for a Bourgeois Life alongside

a water bed

family vacations to Disney World

a minivan with built-in video player

Lisa Frank school supplies

fondue sets

the wooden tree swing

Letter to the Diaspora

Dear Diaspora,

Does memory eat the body?

What is the body whittled down? The eyes as locket, mouth, hinge?

Language cannot express all memory, those that are not wholly present, that exist at the edges, so that you only recall in small moments of brilliance, when someone shows you a picture, a place where you were present and your body took up space, acted and moved and was acted upon and you realize you would never remember your body there if it wasn't for this other to unlock this small part living in you but separate from you. How can this be?

a fish leaping out of the depths   the well

a moment of light

orange flame, brief glimmer, a slice

What if: memory is the light you swallow?

You Google Vietnam

find it in an O C strip mall   Little Saigon   where a man is slapped with a hand full of spit outside his Hi-Tek Video store   Little Saigon   where the man is hit from behind and someone drapes the old flag over his fallen body yellow   three red stripes   *when people see the picture he hung they see blood*   they hang effigies   the man says *I am not a communist   communists killed my brother*   but no one hears him   in his hands he holds a sign that reads   *nothing is more precious than liberty*   thousands stand outside his store for weeks   *we could not do this in our country without getting shot*

Charlie's Angels

Suzi thinks if only she had Lucy Liu's freckles she could be beautiful. She loved her performance in *Charlie's Angels*, the reboot. She now rounds corners with clasped hands, a pointer-finger gun. Every Sunday Mass she prays for high cheekbones and thin face. Last Christmas her cousins started calling her Big Head. It was because her mother had never given birth to her, she knew. She: a C-section baby, sliced out. Yes, if only her face held sharper corners, a pointed diamond, she might finally be someone: *a freckled girl of someone's dreams.*

HAGS

Some days Suzi dots her *i* with an *x*. But in Bobby Frank's yearbook she presses her lips above the *i* so that he will always remember her. She practices a few times first on loose-leaf, her lips sticky with color, her lips parted: a peach halved and pitted. In her room, the walls are shiny with Vaseline kisses before bed.

What Suzi Believes

eating too much ketchup might turn you / pink / some library books / have pages made from recycled toilet / paper / both hands are needed / on the steering wheel / the yellow tape measure she finds / from her mother's tailoring days / is a Burmese python she drapes / across her shoulders / à la Britney Spears / the more she thinks about her mother / or father / dying / the more likely it will happen / God can hear her / thinking of sex / during Sunday Mass / but not when she prays / for her parents' safety / at home / on the way to and from work / the century egg her mother / gifts her / cannot spoil / the sparrows that fly into H Mart / perched on rafters / cannot leave / worse than dying is disappearing

Grief as a Question:

Do you have a permit to sit under the sky?

green is the color of my ecstasy

lying in the roots of a tree, I want to inhale it

everywhere I go I cannot get away

things that glow:

jellyfish   night light   screen saver

the first daffodil to show itself

grass stains   tennis ball

glow-in-the-dark constellations

electric energy drink

key lime sour between teeth

queen moth   praying mantis   inchworm

sour green apple, soft at the bruises

caterpillars taking over roads and sidewalks, placed in jars covered in Saran Wrap
with poked holes for air, a twig and some grass

Virginia fireflies

we caught them and put an eye to our hands making empty fists   shook them

by next morning they no longer glowed

we turned our jars upside down

no one told me grief could be so ordinary

???

The Boat People

She googles F.O.B.

after someone calls her *fresh off the boat.*

She has never been on a boat.

What she finds:

_____ deaths from _____ to _____

___ memorials in __ countries

On open water

They traveled on small fishing junks / origami boats / arms and legs folded /
one over the other / trawlers / smuggling thousands of / bodies / searching
for international / water / living on empty / for weeks and months / looking
for coastline / that did not push back

**Vietnamese Boat People Memorial, Asian Garden of Peaceful Eternity,
Westminster Memorial Park**

The man and old woman / the young mother and child / frozen in bronze /
turned blue-green / four figures so soaked / they have become the water-
logged / wrinkles / of their clothing / four figures on the raft / floating in
a fountain / shaped like the body / of a boat / their bodies submerging /
above water / the young woman's outstretched / hand / reaching back / in
time / around the fountain lay / 54 stones / each inscribed with names /
a small portion / of the dead

The cost of leaving:

24-karat gold bars

bribery

cover of night

Obituaries archives

Obituary 1:

XXX, 16 years old, of _____, drowned on an unknown date sometime after September 1, when he and his family are known to have left their house to meet the People Smugglers. The boat he was on is believed to have been boarded by pirates, who searched passengers for gold sewn into the hemming of their clothes. His younger sister is believed to have been abducted with other young girls onboard. The pirates rammed the small vessel. There were no survivors reported.

Obituary 2:

XXX, 54 years old, of _____, survived for two weeks on a small fishing boat with over 100 passengers before dying from dehydration. Her body was thrown overboard the morning of March 19, and a surviving witness described the scene as "peaceful, almost like she was sleeping." The surviving witness is unsure what happened to the woman's two young children who were also onboard.

Obituary 3:

XXX, 32 years old, of _____, previously served as a low-ranking officer in the ARVN and was interned for over 3 years between 5 different re-education camps. Family members say he grew increasingly hopeless and desperate in the year after his release. He was forcibly relocated to a New Economic Zone where he was to grow his own food on a plot of uninhabitable forest. He continued to live in his mother's house in secret and resorted to hawking cigarettes and rubber tires, a faceless specter of war. The first time the new regime came looking for him, they knocked. The second time they came unannounced: he was alerted by dog cries and escaped out the back door and over 3 fences. He is survived by his mother and three sisters.

Obituary 4:

XXX, 62 years old, of _____, died along with 431 others when their boat capsized on open water. He was a talented pianist, who played for his church congregation, and a journalist. He did not report to the new regime but paid gold to get his immediate family and himself to Campuchia, where they could find short passage to the Thailand coast.

Obituary 5:

XXX, 26 years old, of _____, last seen on the night of June 18, a few hours before his departure for what was to be his seventh attempt to leave the country.

On the boat

people drank urine / licked their palms / of sweat / the tide brought them in / human / cargo / a small island camp / swarming bodies / under palm fronds and scrap metal / waiting to be screened / giving birth to new life / waiting / raising fighting roosters / waiting / waiting five years / can you die of waiting / waiting / denied asylum

Bodies

on hunger / strike / bodies on fire / self-stabbing / in protest of Galang / conditions / bodies imprisoned / after six years / forced returnee

Interview #1

The former Boat Person stated that as many as 20 ships passed by without stopping and coming to their aid, ignoring their cries for help. When they finally saw shore, the refugees sank the boat with their bodies, pounding their hands and feet, so that they could not be towed away.

The People Smugglers speak

They come to us with black-market gold / whole life savings / homes sold / they / the soon-to-be defectors / they will say they are going / on holiday / or nothing at all / they will disappear / in the middle of the night / walk through mud and green jungle / reappear in darkest morning / some commission their own boats built / traveling petri dish / of human / waste / fever dream / we know men who have tried / to leave many times / only to be turned back / bad weather bad feeling / they will not give up / they would squander their life / savings a dozen times / anything for the chance of freedom / the promise of blue ocean

Copy of smuggled letter, ca. 1977

Dear Brother,

I have been lucky. I am good at memorizing lessons and spitting out the ideology they desire. I have not been ill but I am young. I fear for the old. They tire quickly under the sun, the jungle heat. But it is not safe to rest. It is not safe to think for ourselves.

They place us at the bottom of the well for days or shut us into freight containers or ditches. Even with no clear transgressions they leave us there for days, weeks. When I close my eyes, there is only more darkness. But I have been lucky.

Tell Mother not to worry. Tell Mother I am coming home.

According to a statement released by the Vietnamese Foreign Ministry:

"To re-educate them is to help them to realize their crimes, to offer them an opportunity to listen to reason and to reform themselves into honest-minded people, thus contributing to the common cause of national reconstruction."

According to a statement released by Vietnamese government officials:

"After the southern part of Vietnam was liberated, those people who had worked for and cooperated with the former government presented themselves to the new government. Thanks to the policy of humanity, clemency and national reconciliation of the State of Vietnam, these people were not punished.

"Some of them were admitted to re-education facilities in order to enable them to repent their mistakes and reintegrate themselves into the community."

Obituaries archives

Obituary 6:

XXX, 27 years old, of _____, a former low-ranking officer in the ARVN, died while being re-educated from

a) malaria

b) malnutrition

c) dysentery

d) unknown

His family was not notified.

Obituary 7:

XXX, 24 years old, of _____, a former low-ranking officer in the ARVN, suffered for his unwavering repudiation of the new regime. His body was contorted for one week in what is called the Airplane.

Obituary 8:

XXX, 68 years old, of _____, a former doctor conscripted into the army, now a war criminal guilty of national treason, reported for re-education with enough provisions for 10 days as counseled by the new regime. Put on lower rations for using his medical knowledge to treat other prisoners; quickly fell ill. It is unknown what happened to his son, a 21-year-old former soldier, who did not report but attempted to flee by boat.

Interview #2

We had to write mandatory confession multiple times a day. We had to write our life story, including everything we owned, several times a month. If we excluded something we had written previously, we were punished. The more we could confess, even the slightest past misdeeds, the better we thought our chances of freedom. I saw men become mentally incapacitated from the pressure.

Autobiography: a catalogue

Before the war, I lived above my noodle shop with my wife and two young children. My parents died when I was a child. I never met my grandfather or grandmother. My father was not rich, but he made enough money peddling whatever he could sell, and we did not go hungry. Our meals were usually rice and vegetables, the occasional protein. My grandfather, I am told, was a farmer and owned at least 2 water buffaloes, 6 pigs, and many chickens. My father did not own any livestock. My grandfather died of old age, and my parents both died from lung cancer.

My noodle shop earned me good money to feed my family and buy them clothes and other necessities, but I was never rich. I owned no livestock but we had 1 television, 1 radio, 2 beds, 1 fan, 8 pots and pans for the shop, and 1 dresser.

Interview #3

The former refugee stated his assets were taken by the new regime and he was resettled to a New Economic Zone with hundreds of other urban dwellers. Living in the city did not prepare them for collective farming on virgin grounds, and many escaped back to the city. There they became the shadows of war, hiding in the homes of relatives, peddling in the streets.

Confession

In the name of the Father, and of the Son, and of the Holy Spirit. My last confession was today.

I have, in the past, actively worked to cripple the new regime.

I have had harmful thoughts about He Who Enlightens: Our Great Patriot and Uncle.

My war crimes include aiding and abetting the old puppet government, allowing my son to join the puppet war machine, and refusing to report his current whereabouts, which are unknown to me.

I am sorry for these and all the sins of my past life.

Interview #4

We were promised freedoms. Freedom of religion, press, individual thought. We were promised democratic and economic liberties and a halt to corruption.

But the new regime has acted like any other past conqueror in history: power hungry, putting into place reforms that reflect a desire to enact revenge.

Things are different but worse.

Vietnamese Boat People Memorials, Pulau Bidong and Galang

Unveiled March 2005

Front inscription: *"In commemoration of the hundreds of thousands of Vietnamese people who perished on the way to freedom (1975–1996). Though they died of hunger or thirst, of being raped, of exhaustion or of any other cause, we pray that they may now enjoy lasting peace."*

Back inscription (Pulau Bidong): *"In appreciation of the efforts of the UNHCR, the Red Cross and Malaysian Red Crescent Society and other world relief organizations, the Malaysian Government and people as well as all countries of first asylum and resettlement. We also express our gratitude to the thousands of individuals who worked hard in helping the Vietnamese refugees. Overseas Vietnamese Communities, 2005."*

Back inscription (Galang): *"In appreciation of the efforts of the UNHCR, the Red Cross and Indonesian Red Crescent Society and other world relief organizations, the Indonesian Government and people as well as all countries of first asylum and resettlement. We also express our gratitude to the thousands of individuals who worked hard in helping the Vietnamese refugees. Overseas Vietnamese Communities, 2005."*

Destroyed June 2005

It was reported that the Vietnamese government pressured the Malaysian and Indonesian governments, who sanctioned and witnessed the construction and unveiling of the stone memorials, to destroy them.

It was reported that the Malaysian Foreign Affairs Ministry ordered the local government of Pulau Bidong to carry out the memorial's demolition.

It was reported that the memorial in Galang was destroyed without notice.

Interview #5

The former Boat Person stated he escaped with his wife and daughter on a small river boat. His two sons escaped separately. It was common at the time to split your family over multiple trips. The hope was at least one boat made it. If a boat carrying your entire family went down you would lose everyone, he said, miming a boat going under water.

Half of his family still resides in Vietnam, and he sends money every month. He knows of others who have sent back microwaves, chain saws, water pumps, oral contraceptives, and sanitary napkins through a pipeline between Orange County, California, and Vietnam.

"SOME BOAT PEOPLE WILL BE RETURNED"

"We have tried to make it very clear to them: there is no more hope" "The last ones will be the most difficult" "We have gone deep into their hearts to tell them: 'This is the time to go. If you keep delaying, it will only get worse'" "The threat of mandatory repatriation remains" "This is the way, sadly, that deportation is done all over the world" "It is very dangerous, very dangerous to give them hope that they can still go to America" "We are the people who have nothing to come back to, and that's why we stayed there for so long. If I only had a home or a family to come back to, I would have done that a long time ago" "It's a rather sad business" "There has been no question of force" "We will do everything we can to encourage and enable people to return home in dignity. Whether they do so, in the final analysis, depends on their own behavior, which we cannot control" "We must keep the names anonymous because many have indicated that they may be under severe persecution when they return home" "Our people go into the camps under the auspices of the (U.N. High Commissioner for Refugees) to remove any false expectations by non-refugees of having a chance to resettle in America" "She went out to see some friends about nine months ago and never came back. When we heard she had left by boat, we thought they were joking" "We Americans have a special relationship to people who have managed to escape from Vietnam" "There is a limit to our hospitality" "The recent new arrivals are not bona fide refugees" "People in the camps are being given false hopes" "I remember the American bombing, but the memory gets vague. That's why we left" "I am happy to be back in my homeland" "We bring to the American Congress a message of blood and tears with cries for urgent help from people who thirst for freedom like we thirst for sunshine. Save us" "These are our guys. We left them behind"

Can you define a refugee?

A refugee seeks refuge.

Interview #6

I did not want to go back / when they took us / to the plane / it was over very quick / we owned almost nothing still / after 7 years / the men brought their fists / together / desperate / we dragged our feet / refused to walk / threw our bodies / against their barricade / were met with water / cannon / the men were rolled into blankets / loaded into the cabin / like a cigarette in the plane's mouth / a stilled bullet

Vietnamese Boat People Memorial, Captain Burke Park, Kangaroo Point

A mother holds her son's hand / on the other hand / a bird / in midflight / looks at the mother / the boy looks / the other way / it is impossible to tell / which direction is future / which past

???

Smooth Jazz 105.9

In the before-times, Suzi's father picked her up from school in a white Toyota Corolla with duct-taped upholstery and broken passenger-window crank. He listened to talk radio or *Smooth Jazz*, a bag of dried squid ready for her. Suzi crunched with her mouth open, blocking out the radio host with the fuzzy-morning voice. Suzi doesn't like jazz, though when she is interviewed about it for Friday morning video announcements she lies, saying *I love jazz. My father always plays it in the car, so that's how I know.*

Ode to Hunger

Praise SPAM fried with fish sauce and sugar

    jackfruit, 25 lbs. of it carved on newspaper, latex sap sticking fingers

Praise Kraft mac & cheese: small miracle of powdered cheddar

    pork floss in the big Tupperware

    Sara Lee   Praise soy sauce and rice

      shrimp Cup Noodles, 3 minutes 'til done

Praise the soft insides of baguettes

    the first star fruit, pocketed and sliced

      to Chef Boyardee

to durian, sweet scent of garbage

      to pickled mustard greens, Lean Cuisine

      pizza bagels after school

Praise Women, Infants, and Children

    banana blossoms, hearts thinly sliced in vinegar, drained of all color

Dream of Double

i.

Suzi likes to watch her mother get ready.

One stroke or two. Eye shadow, lipstick, blush.

Smokey brown eyes under tattooed brows. *Beautiful.*

ii.

Her mother tapes her eyes wider.

Each sheet of double-sided eyelid tape holds many moons: tapered, transparent, hypoallergenic. She thinks of her cut thumb nails in the sink.

Now her mother's eyelids have deeper creases, and she can see each raised moon like a sickle.

Don't I look younger? More awake?

The packaging promises an end to droopy lids. Promises youth, alertness, dove eyes without the surgery.

iii.

Suzi tries mascara, eyeliner.

Draws a crescent for each brow, separates her lashes with a safety pin despite her fear.

She presses an almond over each eye and squints.

She'd read a story where the main character was a girl like her with almond eyes that narrowed into slants or slits, wore a hood.

What else could her eyes be?

iv.

Magic mirror

Sour lemon

Locket hinging open

The wings of a moth

v.

Whenever Suzi cries too much she wakes up with a swollen face. She is afraid her semi-double lids will never return, stands in front of the bathroom mirror and uses a fingernail to trace the creases back into place over and over and over only to watch them disappear over and over and

vi.

Her mother is good at saving—

Stamps lifted off bills, coupons, spearmint in a damp towel.

She brings home cash nightly, deposits a third into the Bank for Future Funds: unseen stockpile with good intentions: brooding nest egg *in-case-of-emergencies* only.

Suzi is glad that it will never be enough for her mother to go under the knife.

vii.

Suzi is afraid of knives, of all sharp things, afraid that she will close her eyes and blink them open to a new center.

Letter to the Diaspora

Dear Diaspora,

every day I am impatient with language   how slowly it bends to my ear

    one day I hope to speak to my mother   my father

how will I tell them I am falling in love   I am happy   I am becoming someone

        how to speak about language where there is no language

    they speak with their tongues

                        I do not have one

I am 2 parts   fish sauce

1 part lime   juice   sugar dissolving

    a wet match

Suzi Doesn't Miss Her Father

when she remembers how he made her kneel in the hallway or before the front door, the dull carpet marring her knees. Missing someone, she knows, fills you with odd-shaped holes. Suzi remembers her father when she forgets to look both ways before crossing the street or when she steeps oolong for her mother. She remembers his ferocity: slamming his fist on cockroaches, leaving small craters on the table. She doesn't miss getting hit with a wooden ruler, but she wishes now that she could have chosen her own punishment.

You Google Vietnam

The U.S. government refuses to compensate Vietnamese victims of chemical war-
fare because to do so would mean admitting that the U.S. committed war crimes
in Vietnam. This would open the door to lawsuits that would cost the government
billions of dollars.

Fred A. Wilcox, *Scorched Earth*

find 20 million gallons of dioxin   fields of dead   the size of Massachusetts   green
that will never grow back   even the U.S. soldiers did not think   of danger
they showered in the 55-gallon drums   converted them into BBQ pits   *we were aware*
of the potential for damage   everything the mist touched   mangrove fields jungle
camouflage   in war propaganda civilians walk   through deforested canopy
spray themselves with herbicides   *Only you can prevent a forest*

Questions I've Never Asked My Father

i.

do you remember telling me how you and your younger brother competed for first in class

    you were going to be a doctor

when you were sick and missed school you still read the book   still taught yourself

    but the war came

your younger brother didn't have to serve

he's a dentist in France now   the son an engineer   something smart and lucrative

    you work long shifts at the post office   you get one day off

they ask you to come in on the last day of your vacation and you go

    you don't eat lunch because there's no break room

the winter holiday season you work 15-hour shifts

    you fall asleep in your car before making it through the front door

        you fall asleep at the computer checking email

    you sleep through dinner

ii.

when you close your eyes

    what can't you unsee

iii.

who visited you when you were in re-education camp the first time   the second time

Mom said you met bác Tuấn at camp   (which one)

and that's how you met her

        she paid for most dates   she saved up

from her seamstress job

        she wore purple because you loved it most

iv.   did you ever want a boy

        ever know the sex of Mom's miscarriage-after-me

growing up, one of the neighborhood kids asked why you looked so sick

        if it was because you had AIDS

43

I didn't know what to say   how long have you been so skinny

this was the same middle-school kid I saw take his pants off next to the playground

and take a shit on the pavement

the same kid I used to have spitting competitions with

his younger brother got stuck in the bucket-swing meant for infants

the joke was he peed in it

v.

when Veterans Day occurs every year why don't we get to celebrate you and bác Thanh and
bác Tuấn and everyone else who made it to the States

who fought in a war

backed by the U.S.   for the same side

                                                    the same desired outcome

vi.

when you and Mom left Vietnam for America on July 4, 1991

                        did you know the significance of that date

did you know of the long journey yet ahead

44

the fireworks set off every year   a sign of your departure

of the documented arrival   a loud good-bye

when you first landed you lived in bác Thanh's house

generations of children

were raised in that split-level with the rhododendron bushes where I was conceived

much later I heard the stories about anh Nhân and anh Phúc throwing parties

hiding beer in the shrubs   I saw pictures

of chị Linh in her high school graduation cap

after kindergarten when the owner of our small condo wanted us out

you let me decide where to live next

I chose to go back to bác Thanh's house, which was now bác Tuấn's house

you and Mom had a room in the basement

I had a room on the third floor I didn't like to sleep in

when I wanted to lie next to Mom you slept on the ground

vii.

halfway through fourth grade we moved into our townhouse

again you let me choose which one   which school district

which version of American suburbia   this one had a red door

one of the basement storage rooms had been painted to look like a pink tea parlor

one time a salamander tried to burrow itself into the carpeted stairs

Mom and I found its tail sticking out still wriggling

used a dustpan to move it outside

the woods grew into our backyard   deer came forth and ate the flowers we planted

honeysuckle/rose bushes/daylilies/busy lizzies   what would life be

if you'd chosen differently

the one with the blue door   the black railings

Suzi Grows Older

does not fit into her mother's áo dài, it's yellow, her mother wore it at 20, and now Suzi cannot even pull it past her shoulders, not because she is big or fat but because her mother was so thin, a needling needle, an expert embroiderer, deft manicurist, a Very Good Mother, who brought hot cereal in the mornings, the utter safety and love of a damp washcloth on her fevering forehead at 3 a.m.

Suzi Searches for Ecstasy

thinks she'll find it in the back of Bobby Frank's dad's cherry-red BMW but is surprised

instead she finds lollipop wrappers, a pine-scented tree hanging from the mirror that Bobby Frank punches in his excitement to touch her hair

instead she finds his wallet bulging from his jeans

his jeans rough against her thighs, her stomach exposed to the street lamp, his jeans acid-washed and embarrassing

in his hands she wants to be a bird opening its wings, spreading them from car door to car door, she wants to feel the tremor of his throat, to sing through her feathers

but instead the ball of his throat is too angular, the grasp of his hands too large

Suzi searches for ecstasy

hopes she'll find it in her own bedroom where the curtains flap in the month of July, where she is free to watch her own body

where she can spread her fingers to touch the wet light of the moon

where the wet light of the moon casts shadows on the wall

and Suzi can hold the light on the tips of her fingers

Sitting Down with Grief

She calls it anger, love, rapture. Calls it cowardly, ecstatic. Heavy on the chair, grief does not reach the floor, hardly stirs. In its silence, she can hear her own tongue. She examines grief's outline: hazy at best, an in-between color lit from within like an ember of coal. Grief says little: yes, no. Does not say where her father has gone, does not say how to speak the language of her mother.

When it moves, she can feel the start of movement in herself. Two bodies tied to one another with a blade of grass.

Inventory

I don't remember anh Minh and the family chickens   how he always held one   tucked in the
swoop of thin arm

I don't remember him on Halloween   trick-or-treating alone   a trash bag in his hands
carrying out a strange ritual   did he have a costume?   foreigner?   lonely child?

I remember in the backroom   of Theresa's parents' little   trinket shop   putting duct tape
on pubescent legs   ripping the tape off   counting the hairs that stood

I remember carving pumpkins in the basement   leaving the door open so the wind would slam
it shut   until anh Minh came downstairs to tell us off   our pumpkins sat   in the living
room window   rotted before Halloween

I don't remember the man's name   old white-haired   white   and his wife   they came

every Thanksgiving   him in his wheelchair   did I ever know it?   who he was?

bác Thanh's sponsor after   the war   how many of us knew why he came

every year   not the kids chasing each other in jelly shoes   not the ones who   ate the

bread stuffing pumpkin   pie   we were as American as potatoes   in gravy

I don't remember the first time I learned   the word *bitch*   or that my mother's first name

was only one letter off   Bich   I remember Mai in elementary school

when other kids found out her middle name was Bich   they chased her   around

the fenced-in playground   kicking mulch into their shoes   *bitchbitchbitchbitchbitch*

I didn't know to question the meaning of the word   never called my mother any thing   other

than Mom   I used to hug her each night when she came to say good night   say I love you

when did I   stop speaking her name into the dark   in elementary school   when a

neighborhood boy called my dog   bitch   I got mad   that's what she is he said

a female dog   I don't remember the first time someone called me   bitch

bitch-face because my face   fails to look   happy when it is not happy   does not stay open

what power do we give a word   when spoken aloud   what power is there in   keeping

a word safe   soft   hidden   what happens when a name is not   spoken

is forgotten   I don't remember forgetting

She Doesn't Know about the War Times

because her father wouldn't speak about the war times. She knows her father met a man during war times who would later introduce him to her mother. That man is now her uncle. She knows that before war times her father was in college: he liked to camp, play volleyball. After the war times, her father and his family dried areca nuts and betel leaves to sell, to stain teeth black. When her mother biked past on the way to teach preschool, he stood in his doorway and stared. Nothing existed during the war times or before or now, in its aftermath: there is only her father. He is somewhere unknown.

Most Noble, Heroic, and Virgin Lady

Her mother tells her / the legends of women / the Trưng sisters / with their army of mothers and daughters / the first to rebel against the Han / call themselves Queen before drowning / disappearing into the sky / Lady Triệu riding / into battle / on an elephant's head / her breasts a meter long / tied behind her back / these are not fairy tales / her mother says / we are people of war / women / will always sustain us / I have been to their temples / woman means immortal

You Google Vietnam

find the Real-Life Vietnamese Tarzan   his father ran into the jungle in '72   did not
look back at the crater where his home once stood   in the documentary Vietnamese
Tarzan says the world is   *noisy   there is a light at night everywhere*
he carves a hole into bamboo where bats nest   one on top of the other   catches them
in his palm   *You'd never seen light before? Not even from a distance?*
the moon he says   in his outstretched hand is a mother-of-pearl shell   fished from the sea
     no   it is from a *crashed helicopter*   a bowl for eating   he holds out a knife
carved from the dull   steel of U.S. bombs   *what do you think the moon is?   a light*
the people put in the sky   and how can they hang the moon so high?   they hang it up
with a long rope

Letter to the Diaspora

Dear Diaspora,

ecstasy moves through the body quickly

in short quips and yelps

   leaves its aftermath on my tongue

the question: *how to slow it down?*

grief becomes a body of water

      asks *where are your cloves of garlic? your sliced bird's eye chili?*

the body of water wants to be named   is only a girl

ecstasy demands more

     taste buds adjusting to the taste of hunger

   my body risking itself

Suzi as a Series of Questions:

Did Father ever return? Why did he leave?

How did Mother pay her hospital bills?

Who escorted me home?

When did I first notice my body?

How am I always silent?

What was in the green light?

Mother showed me

because I left the stove on

because I stole flowers from the altar

because I did not receive Communion

he was large

    and took from my body

        the ground pressed rocks into my back

blades of green around my neck

        in this memory, I am small

the body is loud

sometimes Mother speaks

to me in a life I don't

    remember and I can see

it makes her sad

when I can't answer

     I try to speak

anyway, but English

is what makes her sad

    I fall back into the shape

of my mouth

I can never remember falling asleep, but I can always remember my dreams: last night I could walk on water and the salted sea carried me to my father's shadow. It carried me to an inlet where butterflies drifted though milkweed. I stayed away from their terrible bodies.

I don't know

In a Past Life

mother was a preschool teacher / 5 a.m. churchgoer / outside her house grand-
father cut hair / to his right was grandmother selling / firework powder /
air drying fish bought in Vũng Tàu / and bused back on grandmother's lap / in
a past life / mother ran up and down / the stairs / to stoke the ten-hour fire /
burning under glutinous rice / after '75 she was bused to a field / stepped bare-
foot / into mud / dug irrigation systems / afraid of what she might step on /
when grandfather fell / no one knew the word *stroke* / grandmother rubbed
oil on his hands and feet / sold MSG / in a past life / mother woke up /
to the sound of cyclos / notching the roads / when grandmother / died /
mother flew back and tied white / linen around her head / in mourning

*It was not like the first time on the plane when they served packets of peanut
butter and jelly. Concord grape. I stole dozens. I did not know if I would see
them again.*

Unending

I am learning how to hold grief
in my mouth. Something alive

until it isn't. Like a field is a field
until it isn't, until it is just the color green.

Listen when I tell you how a field
folds into a clover when I am on my hands,

how the memory of what I am looking
for is not as important as the ground

it claims. I don't mean that grief
can be unalive. Or that I keep it loaded

in that place between lower lip
and teeth. I mean I never walked the land

where my father harvested seeds.
In his field, he waited for green

to bend into gold. A single blade
splitting light until there was nothing else.

My father remembers. I watch my shadow.

ACKNOWLEDGMENTS

Sincere gratitude to the editors of the following publications in which some of these poems have appeared, sometimes in different forms.

The Shallow Ends: "The First Language"
Glass: A Journal of Poetry: "Most Noble, Heroic, and Virgin Lady"
Tin House: "In a Past Life"
DIAGRAM: "The Body as a Series of Questions:"
Nimrod: "Beast Angel" and "If I Say My Body Is Grieving"
Action, Spectacle: "Unending"

Thank you to Kwame Dawes, Matthew Dickman, Kate Daniels, and Hilda Raz for seeing something in my work. I still can't quite believe it.

Thank you to the team at the University of Nebraska Press for taking such good care of my manuscript and helping me usher it into the world, especially Kwame Dawes, Ashley Strosnider, Courtney Ochsner, Rosemary Sekora, and Elizabeth Zaleski. To you, my gratitude knows no bounds.

Thank you to my teachers, mentors, and friends at Arizona State University for the never-ending support. Thank you to my students for placing trust in me and for teaching me what I don't know. Norman Dubie, Sally Ball, and Alberto Ríos: this book would not be possible without you. I cherish your kindness and generosity. Thank you, Xu Xi, for encouraging me to take classes outside of the MFA. Cảm ơn cô Kim for teaching me how to be vulnerable in language.

Thank you to Natalie Diaz for challenging me to expand my lexicon for grief and tenderness and ecstasy. For showing me how to think critically and imagine freely. For teaching me how to advocate for myself and ask. This book and my poet heart are better because of you.

Thank you to the team at the Virginia G. Piper Center for Creative Writing, especially to Angie Dell for all of the help and support over the years, and to Felicia Zamora for the fierce encouragement to believe in myself.

Thank you to everyone with whom I crossed paths and who inspired, uplifted, and energized me in so many ways. Thank you to Maritsa Leyva for doing all of this from day one. Thank you to my MFA cohort for your kinship. Joel Salcido, Rashaad Thomas, and Jake Friedman, for the love you put into building community and for holding the door open for others. Scott Daughtridge DeMer and Stephanie Dowda DeMer, for the work you do in creating space for artists and for inviting me to read alongside wonderful writers at the Letters Festival. Erika Meitner, for encouraging my poet heart in the early days and for giving me advice on MFAs. Cathy Linh Che, for all the shared wisdom.

Thank you to the following organizations, which have supported me and my imagination in so many ways: the Virginia G. Piper Center for Creative Writing for the numerous awards and fellowships, including the Glendon and Kathryn Swarthout Awards in Writing, the Aleida Rodriguez Memorial Award in Creative Writing, and the Creative Research Fellowship that led to the beginnings of an oral history project, the fruits of which appear throughout this collection; Idyllwild Arts, especially Victoria Chang for the time you spent with me and my words; the Arizona Commission on the Arts for the Opportunity Grant for Artists that enabled my body to wander and create on Oregon's wet coast; Tin House, especially Lance Cleland and India Downes-Le Guin for creating a welcoming space, and Gabrielle Calvocoressi for the tenderness and care with which you led workshop.

Thank you to everyone I have met and loved along the way. Thank you to the writers and artists before me who helped me find myself in art and learn that a body like mine can be held, nourished.

Thank you, Sören. My first reader and my partner in all things. For keeping my heart and mind and stomach full.

Thank you to my family. My parents, cousins, aunts, uncles, grandparents, and those I was never lucky enough to meet. Thank you for my survival, my futurity. I am a storyteller because of you.

Cảm ơn bố mẹ. For everything.

SOURCE ACKNOWLEDGMENTS

"Beast Angel" is after Eduardo C. Corral's poem "To the Beastangel."

"If I Say My Body Is Grieving" is after Athena Farrokhzad's *White Blight*.

"You Google Vietnam (find it in an O C strip mall)" borrows and alters language from online articles about the 1999 Little Saigon protests.

"Grief as a Question:" borrows a line from *Journal of an Ordinary Grief* by Mahmoud Darwish.

In "The Boat People":

"According to a statement released by the Vietnamese Foreign Ministry" and "According to a statement released by Vietnamese government officials" quote statements made by the Vietnamese Foreign Ministry and Vietnamese government officials.

"Vietnamese Boat People Memorials, Pulau Bidong and Galang" quotes inscriptions from the Vietnamese Boat People Memorials in Pulau Bidong and Galang.

"'SOME BOAT PEOPLE WILL BE RETURNED'" is composed entirely of brief quotations from numerous articles. The title comes from a 1990 *New York Times* article.

Many of the obituaries are inspired by real-life accounts found during my research on the Vietnamese Boat People.

"You Google Vietnam (find 20 million gallons of dioxin)" borrows language from articles about Agent Orange. It quotes a 1988 letter from James Clary, a scientist who worked for the Chemical Weapons Branch of the Air Force Armament Development Laboratory. The epigraph is a quote from Fred A. Wilcox, author of *Scorched Earth: Legacies of Chemical Warfare in Vietnam*, to *VnExpress International*, a Vietnamese news outlet.

"Most Noble, Heroic, and Virgin Lady" is based on the legend of the sister warriors Trưng Trắc and Trưng Nhị (Hai Bà Trưng) and the legend of Bà Triệu. The title comes from a transliteration of one of Bà Triệu's given titles and was found on Wikipedia.

"You Google Vietnam (find the Real-Life Vietnamese Tarzan)" borrows and alters language from articles and videos about Hồ Văn Lang. Over four decades after the war's end, he and his father were found living deep in the jungle with no outside contact with civilization.

To order or obtain more information on these or other University of Nebraska Press titles, visit nebraskapress.unl.edu.

CPSIA information can be obtained
at www.ICGtesting.com
Printed in the USA
LVHW040144120523
746752LV00004B/787